Copyright 2024
All ri

Copyrighted material.

I dedicate this poetry book to my parents
Billy and Trudy (Murray) Kavanagh.
They have taught me from a young age
to appreciate nature in all her glory.

CONTENTS

A SPLASH OF SUNLIGHT.	4
A DANCE WITH A SWAN.	5
A HOWLING NIGHT IT IS.	6
AS THE RAIN FALLS.	7
FLY BIRD FLY.	8
I RETURN TO MY TREES.	9
JUST A LITTLE HOUSE BESIDE THE LAKE.	10
MAKE YOUR HEARTBEAT MATCH WITH THE BEAT OF NATURE.	11
SURROUNDED BY SUCH BEAUTY.	12
THE BEAUTY OF NATURE.	13
THE COLD NIGHT AIR.	14
THE DOVE.	15
THE LITTLE FOX.	16
THE MAGIC OF NATURE.	17
THE MAGICAL BEAUTY OF WINTER.	18
THE OLD OAK.	19
THE WIND IS BLOWING HARSHLY AGAINST MY WINDOW PANE.	20
WINTER GIVES WAY TO SPRING.	21
THERE WAS A WHISPER OF SUNSHINE.	22
WITHIN THE SHADOW OF THE SUN.	23
AT THE END OF SUMMER.	24
DAYLIGHT COMES AND THEN IT GOES.	25
IN THE LONELINESS OF THE NIGHT.	26
THE EVENING.	27

A splash of sunlight.

A splash of sunlight,
a golden hue.
A dash of orange,
shining through.

A splinter of red,
a stream of gold.
A string of light beams,
glistening so bold.

Without your light,
what would we do.
Without your warmth
it would be so cruel.

Go on shining.
Light up our world.
Let us appreciate,
your unspoken word.

A splash of sunlight,
a golden hue.
A dash of orange,
shining through.

A dance with a swan.

A dance with a swan,
a majestic glide.
A dance with a swan,
where two worlds collide.

The long neck of pride.
The snowy white wings so mild.
The glorious glare.
The dance of dare.

Swirling and splashing around.
Twirling and gaining ground.
Gaining heights of ecstasy.
Listening to every sound.

A dance with a swan,
a majestic glide.
A dance with a swan,
Until nights tide.

A howling night it is.

The storm is brewing high.
The tall oak sways
from left to right.
The moon it gleams in the sky.

Small branches fall to the ground.
They are swept away by the rains water.
The birds fly to shelter under the rooftops.
They do not falter.

As the rain lashes against the window,
I hear a sound in the far distance.
A howling sound that has always fascinated me,
for it is proof of their existence.

I have never seen them about,
But on nights like this,
their spirit is alive and well,
and it brings me bliss.

So a howling night it is.
By candlelight I go to bed.
I listen to their majestic sound.
I listen to all that is said.

As the rain falls down.

As the rain falls down heavily,
and washes everything away.
The dark sky brightens up
with flashes of lightening as if to say
"Hurry up, go on home, do not stay"
And as the water takes away the leaves and all the decay,
the shores are brimming full
and must be emptied without delay.

The trees are blowing fiercely and they sway.
Everything is wet and dreary including me.
My umbrella blows inside out
and then away, I see.

Of home I go or at least I try to.
I am blown from left to right as I cross the road.
The rain pelts down some more,
oh what a down pour.

Home at last, I take of my wet clothes.
A nice hot cup of tea should do the trick.
Looking out the window as the rain falls,
glad to be inside these four walls.

Fly bird fly.

Fly bird fly,
Up to the sky,
Up to the heavens above.
Fly bird fly,
Up to the sky,
Up to the other doves.

Soar and glide,
Flap and slide,
Fly fast and free.
Never again in a cage.
Never again with me.

I set you free
as I am.
Never again bound.
Fly bird fly up to the sky.
And let me hear your sound.

I return to my trees.

I return to my trees
and the heavens above me.
I return to all I had forgotten
and all I had not seen.

I understand more each meaning.
I realise what I had closed my eyes to,
and now my walls are not blocked.
My heart is unlocked.

I know that in life we need a balance,
for everything to work.
But we also need to face things
and not cover up what lurks.

I return to my trees
and the heavens above me.
I return to their beauty
and their undying love.

Dod yn ol at fy nghoed.

Just a little house beside the lake.

Just a little house beside the lake
is where I want to live
Where the mountains touch the sky
and show the beauty that they give.
Where the water is so blue and icy clear.
Where the goats run down the hills and
where the poppies bloom so near.

Where each day is filled with laughter
and each night with sheer delight.
The land of the midnight sun
in the summer, no need for candlelight.

And in the winter to curl up with a book,
the embers of the fire,
dance brightly with every look,
and with every known desire.

Yes to the little house beside the lake
where time stood still.
Where home will be and always will.

Make your heartbeat match with the beat of nature.

Make your heartbeat match
with the beat of nature.
Lift your face to the sun
and embrace its rays.
Smell the enticing aroma
of the beautiful roses,
that adorn this wonderful place.

Listen to the blackbird singing joyously
in the magnificent oak.
Watch the bumble bee dance amongst the
luminous petals.
See the clouds drift by on a breezy day.
Enjoy the lambs playing in the fields
of newly cut hay.

At night, look to the stars,
sparkling and celestial.
Listen to the howl of the Wolf,
as the Full Moon beams in the sky.
Notice the deer as he eats the shrubs that are essential.
See the hare as he runs on by.

Make your heartbeat match
the beat of nature.
Lift your face to the sun
and embrace its rays
Smell the enticing aroma of the
beautiful roses,
that adorn this wonderful place.

Surrounded by such beauty.

Surrounded by such beauty,
that brings joy to my heart.
The everending peace and calm,
with one look around imparts.

Each day brings new things to look at,
new things to explore.
The wondrous wealth of nature,
comes pleasantly to my door.

Every little bird that sings,
every swish of a leaf in the breeze.
Every flap of an eagles wing,
Every drop of the sunlight that please.

The magnificent colours of blue,
that stretch over a wondrous sky.
The soft moss under my feet,
leads me gently way on by.

To live another day
surrounded by such beauty.
All my wishes combined
and with it comes a duty.

To protect all that I see.
To let it flourish.
The beauty that surrounds me,
is something to love and nourish.

The beauty of nature.

The beauty of nature,
I see it every day.
In all the seasons and months
its loveliness does lay,
in every tiny bud,
in every tiny seed,
in every tiny insect,
if we were to heed.

But we are so busy that we forget
to see the beauty around us.
Always rushing, always looking in our phones,
Never paying attention even when we are alone.

The beauty of nature
shines its light on our world.
Let us protect it.
Let us keep our word.

The cold night air.

The cold night air,
is all you knew.
The icy waters and
the morning dew.

Your howls could be heard
from the mountain high.
The snow blew east,
across the sky.

The stars they shone,
and I could see,
the path you took,
led straight to me.

Come my friend,
your visit is overdue.
I have missed your presence.
your honest view.

The cold night air,
is all you knew.
The icy waters and the
morning dew.

The dove.

The dove of peace and light,
that flies so softly by.
The dove that makes things right,
in a world of dismay and lies.

Your calmness gives us hope.
Your strenght uplifts our souls.
We continue our journey
for we now know our goals.

And now when we look in the mirror,
and we can truly see,
what we tried to hide and not face.
What we can really be.

Peace will come to our world
when the lust for power ceases.
Until we understand this fact,
Everything will always be in pieces.
For peace within ourselves, spreads to all others.
No more fighting our demons.
No more running for cover.

So little dove fly by so peacefully high.
You are a sign of hope and love,
that will come in time.

The little fox.

Little fox sleep.
Dream fast in your slumber.
Little fox do not weep.
The day is long.
You will have many adventures
to sing about when it is over.

The forest is your playground.
Deliciously green.
Scouting around for your prey.
To be inevidently seen.

Down by the stream.
The salmon leaps.
Glistening water trickles.
Down in the deep.

Little fox sleep.
Dream fast in your slumber.
Little fox do not weep.
The day is not over.

The magic of nature.

When I disappear on my woodland walk,
and I blend amongst the trees,
all the little things I see,
all these do please.

I soak everything in,
including the sun.
A light breeze sways by,
whilst I am having fun.

The leaves of the oak,
hold a few drops of glistening dew.
A squirrel scurries slowly down
and stops to view.

The moss under my feet is so soft
like an old carpet,
and all kinds of wild mushrooms
mostly surround it.

At last I come to the stream.
The sound of running water
is pleasing to ones ears.
The salmon takes a leap
And with it brings much cheer.

The magic of nature surrounds me,
what would I be without it.
It would be a very cold and dark place to live.
Nothing could ever replace it.

The magical beauty of winter,

The magical beauty of winter,
is displayed on every snowy branch.
The snow glistens like diamonds,
and puts you in a trance.

The icy glare of the lake.
The foggy dew of the sky.
The water trickling along.
The silver clouds slowly going by.

The houses in the distance,
with their Christmas lights.
The church bell rings,
What a delight.

The snow is coming down.
Like cottonwool from the sky.
The sky is getting dark.
Its time to say goodbye.

The old oak.

The old oak, it stands there,
like it has for hundreds of years.
It has seen many people walk by,
foxes and deers.

It has seen so many buildings go up
and so many come down.
It has seen so many smiles
and even as many frowns.

It has felt the soft flowing breeze
between its branches,
the warm sun on a summers day.
The icy snowy flakes in winter.
The first buds that come in May.

The old oak it stands there,
I hope it will last many more years.
Bringing beauty to my street
and some happy cheer.

The wind is blowing harshly against my window pane.

The wind is blowing harshly against my window pane.
Its sound is rough and daunting,
as it whistles through the lane.
The old oak tree outside is swaying to and fro.
The leaves are swirling past,
not really knowing where to go.

The little blackbird finds shelter under the bush.
The majestic swan is gliding,
not even in a rush.
Now the clouds are fiercely taking over the sky.
The birds disappear till
everything calms down,
at least they try.

And in the midst of the storm,
the sun suddenly appears.
Its light shines down so heavenly,
on the rains tears.

The wind is calmer now,
no more loud noise.
You can hear the seagulls in the distance,
you can hear their screeching voice.

The wind is blowing harshly against my window pane.
Its sound is rough and daunting,
as it whistles through the lane.
I am quite content to be inside
and listen to the rain.
Knowing that afterwards,
everything is going be the same.

Winter gives way to spring.

Winter gives way to spring.
It gives way to freshly born buds.
It gives way to a fresh cool breeze.
The death of winter, the freezing cold, the blusterous winds,
disappeared under the mantle of a beautiful spring day.

The birds started chirping early in the morning.
The lambs bleating on the hillside, playfully running
through the grass full of primroses and daffodils.

The darkness was gone.
Banished away till next autumn.
You could hear the joy in the air.
People chattering as they went by,
on their way to market.

Oh please let it be Spring all year round.
It is my favourite time of year.
The time of rebirth and growth.
The time of revitalisation after the stagnation of winter.
Let my dream come true.

There was a whisper of sunshine.

There was a whisper of sunshine,
when the birds flew away.
As the cold crisp air blew in,
I felt a little warmth on that day.

I was busy reading books,
that had piled up over the years.
I had no time before,
was always busy with those near.

So now I had sometime
to catch up with my first love, reading,
how I had forgotten,
how much enjoyment it was feeding.

When I was younger I could read for days,
everything from ghost stories to murder mysteries.
As the suns rays shone lightly on my head
I revelled in every page that I read.

Soon it was time to head home to bed.
I had made a promise to myself that day.
Even on days were there was never a whisper of sunshine,
I would make time to read always.

Within the shadow of the sun.

Within the shadow of the sun,
stood all things that were not clear.
And even if the light whispered tenderly
through the branches,
it did not reveal the real truth.

What was hidden stayed hidden,
till morning light,
When the sun shone fiercely
and all colours of crimson red and marmelade orange lit up the valley,
as if it was on fire.

Within the shadow of the sun
you can hide,
but not forever.
It will find you one day and
reveal your true colours.

At the end of summer.

At the end of summer,
as I sit in the long grass,
surrounded by butterflies
and thoughts of you.

The sun slowly disappears,
and the stars come out one by one,
twinkling brightly as the blue moon peers.

I love to sleep in the grass
and look up to the night sky.
A hare appears and goes to sleep under the tree.
A deer gracefully runs by.

Soon fall will come and winter too,
Bringing back memories that I remember with joy,
when I had hope in my heart.
But that hope is gone now,
Like the spring.
I wonder what the fall will bring.

Daylight comes and then it goes.

Daylight comes and then it goes,
and nothing ever seems to change.
I have my dreams.
I have my hopes.
But they are not within range.

Its hard to feel,
in an unfeeling world,
where no one understands.
The path I go on
is never straight,
but follows different strands.

I wish things could be different,
I really do,
But thats not the case for me.
The daylight comes and then it goes
and reveals what I need to see.

In the loneliness of the night.

In the loneliness of the night.
when everything is quiet,
and all you hear is the wind,
tapping lightly on your window pane,
remember what we had,
even if you are sad,
for our memories, they were good,
We grew and we understood.

As with everything in life,
there is no wrong or right.
The situations are there,
sometimes created by despair.
But you learn if you choose.
You have nothing to lose.
Carry on with your day.
Be happy, come what may.

In the loneliness of the night,
when everything is quiet,
and all you hear is the last geese
flying on its way.
And the morning light appears,
it rises and does not fear.
What lays ahead will come,
but we will face it anyway.

The evening.

The final leaf has fallen now.
The darkness is setting in from afar.
I hear the last goose fly overhead.
It goes to lands beyond our stars.
The winter has reared her head again.
The summer just a memory now.
What is gone before is lost then found.
As I sit here drinking tea and looking all around.
The lights come on, in the street outside.
They flicker and then they become brilliantly bright.
A black cat roams looking for its prey.
The best time to look at the end of the day.
Time to sleep, time to dream.
Time is flying by it seems.
Tomorrow morning awaits.
Hopefully with its bright blue sky and yellow sun beams.

Made in the USA
Columbia, SC
02 March 2025

54574586R00015